The Wedding

Your Wedding day, planned your way. Elaborate or simple, it's up to you.

Sandra Carusi

© **Copyright 2024 - All rights reserved.**

The content contained within this book may not be reproduced, duplicated or transmitted without direct written permission from the author or the publisher.

Under no circumstances will any blame or legal responsibility be held against the publisher, or author, for any damages, reparation, or monetary loss due to the information contained within this book, either directly or indirectly.

Legal Notice:

This book is copyright protected. It is only for personal use. You cannot amend, distribute, sell, use, quote or paraphrase any part, or the content within this book, without the consent of the author or publisher.

Disclaimer Notice:

Please note the information contained within this document is for educational and entertainment purposes only. All effort has been executed to present accurate, up to date, reliable, complete information. No warranties of any kind are declared or implied. Readers acknowledge that the author is not engaged in the rendering of legal, financial, medical or professional advice. The content within this book has been derived from various sources. Please consult a licensed professional before attempting any techniques outlined in this book.

By reading this document, the reader agrees that under no circumstances is the author responsible for any losses, direct or indirect, that are incurred as a result of the use of the information contained within this document, including, but not limited to, errors, omissions, or inaccuracies.

Table of Contents

INTRODUCTION 1

CHAPTER 1: ENVISIONING YOUR PERFECT DAY 3

    DREAM BOARD CREATION 3
        Step 1: Choose Your Tools 3
        Step 2: Gather Inspiration 4
        Step 3: Place and Arrange 4
        Visual Inspiration Sources 5
        Organizing the Board 6
        Using Digital Tools 7
    CULTURAL AND FAMILY TRADITIONS 7
        Talk to Family Members 8
    WEDDING THEMES AND STYLES 8
        Rustic 9
        Modern 9
        Boho 9
        Vintage 9
        Glam 9
        Maintaining Thematic Consistency 10
        Personalizing Popular Themes 10
    THE SIGNIFICANCE OF COLOR SCHEMES 10
        Emotional Impact 10
        Visual Harmony 10
        Color Psychology 11
        Seasonal Color Choices 11
        Coordinating Colors With the Wedding Party 11

CHAPTER 2: BUDGETING AND FINANCING YOUR WEDDING 13

    ESTABLISHING A BUDGET FRAMEWORK 13
        Step-by-Step Budget Framework 14
    COST-SAVING TIPS FOR BIG-TICKET ITEMS 14
        Implementing Cost-Saving Strategies 14
        Additional Tips for Cost Management 15
    UNDERSTANDING WEDDING COSTS 16
        Hidden Costs 16
    PRACTICAL STEPS FOR BUDGETING 16
        Research Specific Costs 16
        Account for Hidden Fees 17
        Consider Off-Peak Discounts 17
        Regular Budget Reviews 17
        Detailed Record-Keeping 17
    DIY VERSUS PROFESSIONAL SERVICES: MAKING INFORMED DECISIONS FOR YOUR WEDDING 18
        DIY Approach 18
        Practical Tips for DIY Success 19
        Professional Services 20
        Practical Steps for Choosing Professional Services 21
    DECIDING BETWEEN DIY AND PROFESSIONAL SERVICES: A BALANCED APPROACH 21
        Identify Priorities 21
        Assess Skills 21

 Budget Analysis 21
 Hybrid Approach 21
 Practical Steps to Implement Your Decision 22

CHAPTER 3: ORGANIZING THE DETAILS 23
 Venue Selection Criteria 23
  Contracts and Negotiations 23
  Tips for Successful Negotiations 24
 Vetting and Selecting Vendors 25
 Guest List Management 25
  Seating Arrangements 27
 Ceremony Planning 27
  Timing and Flow of the Ceremony 29

CHAPTER 4: PERSONAL TOUCHES AND MEMORABLE EXPERIENCES 33
 Personalized Vows and Ceremony Rituals 33
  Vow Writing Workshops 33
  Meaningful Symbols 33
  Tips for Writing and Delivering Vows 34
  Unity Ceremonies 34
  Tips for Unity Ceremonies 36
  Creating Lasting Memories 36
 Signature Cocktails and Menu Customization 36
  Seasonal and Local Ingredients 37
  Themed Menus and Drinks 37
  Tasting Sessions 37
  Crafting an Unforgettable Dining Experience 37
 Cultural Fusions 38
  Bilingual Elements 38
 Interactive Guest Activities 38
  DIY Cocktail Bar 40
  Craft Corner 40
  Memory Lane 40
  Interactive Games 41
  Live Entertainment 41

CHAPTER 5: STAYING SANE: MANAGING STRESS AND ENJOYING THE JOURNEY 43
 Stress Management Techniques 43
 The Role of Support Systems 43
  Delegation Roles 44
  Communication Channels 44
  Professional Help 44
 Last-Minute Troubleshooting 44
  Emergency Kit Preparation 44
  Vendor Backup Plans 45
  Mental Preparedness 46
 Reflecting and Celebrating 47
  Journaling the Journey 47
  Celebratory Rituals 47
  Staying Connected With Your Partner 48
  Embracing the Journey 48

CONCLUSION 49

REFERENCES 51

Introduction

You and your partner step into your wedding venue, and every detail, from the soft glow of the candles to the choice of music, feels like an extension of your heart. As you walk down the aisle together, the faces of your loved ones light up, sharing in the joy of a day that is unmistakably yours. This is not just a dream—it's a reality waiting to be crafted with a bit of guidance and a lot of creativity. Welcome to a world where your wedding day is designed exactly as you both envision it, whether you dream of an elaborate celebration or a simple, intimate gathering.

This is your compass on this exciting journey, empowering you to plan a wedding that truly reflects your personal tastes. More importantly, it's about enjoying every step of the process, turning what can often be a stressful time into a joyful and fulfilling experience for both of you.

In these pages, you'll find the tools and inspiration to create a wedding that is aesthetically pleasing but also deeply meaningful and personal. My mission is to help you design a day that feels like an authentic expression of your love story, whether that means a grand affair with all the trimmings or a minimalist celebration with your closest friends and family.

Here's a glimpse of what you can expect as you dive into this book:

- **Practical advice**: We provide step-by-step guidance on every aspect of wedding planning, from choosing the perfect venue to finalizing the guest list.

- **Personalization tips**: Discover how to infuse personal touches into every element of your wedding, ensuring it's a true reflection of both of you.

- **Budgeting strategies**: Learn tips and tricks to manage your finances effectively, helping you achieve your dream wedding without breaking the bank.

- **Stress management techniques**: Find tools and advice to keep the planning process as stress-free as possible, allowing you to focus on the joy of the journey.

- **Unique ideas**: Get inspired with unique elements that make your wedding stand out, whether it's through creative decor, unconventional venues, or personalized vows.

This is not about adhering to tradition for tradition's sake. Instead, it's about making your own rules and celebrating your unique love story. I encourage you to think outside the box, embrace what truly makes you both happy, and keep an open mind. Together, we'll explore the fun and interactive journey of wedding planning.

Let me share a quick story. I once helped a couple plan a wedding that took place in a forest clearing at sunset. They wanted something magical but intimate, and every detail—from the fairy lights strung between trees to the acoustic guitar music—reflected their love for nature and each other. It was a day that none of their guests will ever forget, and it all started with a clear vision and the willingness to break away from the ordinary.

By the end of this book, you'll have all the tools you need to create a wedding day that's as extraordinary and unique as your love story. So let's embark on this journey together and turn your vision into a beautiful reality.

Chapter 1:

Envisioning Your Perfect Day

Welcome to the first step of your wedding planning journey: envisioning your perfect day. This chapter is all about tapping into your creativity and imagination to articulate and refine a vision that captures your deepest desires and unique personality. Before you dive into the logistics and details, it's essential to create a clear picture of what you want your wedding to look and feel like.

This chapter will guide you through defining the key elements of your wedding day. We will explore themes, styles, and moods to help you narrow down your preferences. You'll learn how to create a cohesive look and feel that ties everything together, from the invitations to the décor and beyond.

Dream Board Creation

Creating a dream board for your wedding is an inspiring and practical way to visualize and refine the vision of your special day. By capturing and organizing your ideas in one place, you can clearly see how all the elements come together, making it easier to communicate your vision to others and stay focused throughout the planning process. Here's how to create a dream board that truly captures your wedding dreams:

Step 1: Choose Your Tools

First, decide whether you want to create a physical or digital dream board. Both have their benefits, so choose the one that best fits your style and needs.

- **Physical dream board:** A corkboard or poster board can be a tactile and engaging way to bring your vision to life. You'll be able to pin, tape, or glue images, fabric swatches, and other tangible items that inspire you.

- **Digital dream board:** Platforms like Canva, Pinterest, or other design software provide a versatile and easily shareable way to compile your ideas. Digital boards are great for organizing a wide range of online resources and can be easily updated as your vision evolves.

Step 2: Gather Inspiration

Begin collecting items that resonate with your dream wedding. This can include:

- **Images:** Look for pictures of venues, décor, floral arrangements, dresses, and other elements that catch your eye. Magazines, websites, and social media are excellent sources of inspiration.

- **Quotes and words:** Find quotes, song lyrics, or even single words that encapsulate the emotions and themes you want for your wedding day.

- **Color swatches:** Collect color samples that you love, which can help guide your choices for flowers, attire, and decorations.

- **Textures and materials:** Fabric swatches, ribbons, or paper samples can add a tactile element to your board, helping you envision the overall aesthetic.

Step 3: Place and Arrange

Once you have gathered your materials, it's time to arrange them on your board. Here's how to do it effectively:

- **Start with a focal point:** Choose a central image or item that represents the core of your wedding vision. This could be a picture of your dream venue, a stunning centerpiece, or a piece of artwork that embodies your theme.

- **Create sections:** Divide your board into sections based on different aspects of the wedding, such as attire, décor, venue, and special moments. This helps organize your thoughts and ensures that all elements are considered.

- **Balance and flow:** Arrange your items in a way that feels balanced and cohesive. Ensure there is a natural flow from one section to the next, reflecting how you envision the day unfolding.

- **Refine and edit:** Don't be afraid to move things around or remove items that no longer fit your vision. This process of refinement will help you hone in on what truly matters.

A dream board helps crystallize your vision, making it easier to make decisions that align with your goals. Share your board with your partner, wedding planner, and vendors to ensure everyone is on the same page. Keep your board in a place where you can see it regularly. It will serve as a constant source of inspiration and motivation as you plan your wedding.

Visual Inspiration Sources

Finding inspiration for your dream wedding can be an exciting journey filled with endless possibilities. Here are some fantastic sources where couples can discover ideas and imagery to fuel their creativity and create stunning dream boards:

- **Magazines:** Wedding magazines are timeless sources of inspiration, where you'll find themes and styles that resonate with you.

- **Pinterest:** Create boards dedicated to different aspects of your wedding, such as attire, décor, and color schemes. Explore a vast array of pins, ranging from DIY projects and budget-friendly hacks to luxury wedding trends and celebrity-inspired looks.

- **Instagram:** Follow wedding-related hashtags like *#weddinginspiration*, *#bridetobe*, or *#weddingdetails* to discover the latest trends and creative ideas.

- **Real Wedding Blogs:** Gain insights from couples who have been in your shoes and learn from their experiences, successes, and challenges.

- **Expos and Shows:** Attend these events to immerse yourself in the world of weddings, explore different options, and gather inspiration firsthand. Chat with vendors, sample products, and collect brochures and business cards to reference later.

With so many visual inspiration sources at your fingertips, there's no shortage of ideas to fuel your creativity and bring your dream wedding to life. Take advantage of these diverse resources to explore different styles, discover new trends, and ultimately define a vision that reflects your unique love story and personality. Let your imagination run wild as you curate your dream board, and watch as your wedding vision evolves into a beautiful reality.

Organizing the Board

Maintaining clarity and focus on your dream board is essential to ensure that it accurately reflects your wedding vision and guides you effectively throughout the planning process. Here are some strategies to organize and refine your board:

Categorize

Organize images and ideas on your dream board by categorizing them according to themes, colors, moods, or types of décor. This helps streamline your vision and makes it easier to visualize how different elements will come together on your wedding day. For example, you could create sections for ceremony décor, reception details, floral arrangements, and attire. Grouping similar items creates a cohesive and harmonious visual representation of your dream wedding.

Prioritize

Highlight elements that are most important to you and your partner on your dream board. Whether it's a specific color palette, a particular style of venue, or a must-have floral arrangement, make sure these key elements stand out prominently. Use larger images, bold colors, or unique accents to draw attention to the aspects of your wedding that you prioritize above all else. By focusing on what truly matters to you, you can ensure that your wedding reflects your values, preferences, and personalities.

Refine

Regularly update and refine your dream board as your vision evolves and your wedding plans take shape. Remove items that no longer align with your vision or that you've decided against incorporating into your wedding. Editing your board helps maintain clarity and prevents it from becoming cluttered or overwhelming. As you make decisions and finalize details, update your board accordingly to ensure that it remains an accurate reflection of your dream wedding. By refining your board regularly, you can stay focused on what truly matters and avoid getting sidetracked by unnecessary distractions.

Use your board as a visual guide to inform your decisions, communicate your ideas to vendors and planners, and ensure that every aspect of your wedding aligns with your vision. As you work toward bringing your dream wedding to life, let your organized and refined dream board serve as a source of inspiration, motivation, and guidance. With clarity and focus, you can create a wedding day that exceeds your wildest dreams and captures the essence of your love story.

Using Digital Tools

Digital tools and apps offer convenient and versatile ways to create and share electronic dream boards, allowing you to visualize and refine your wedding vision with ease. Here are some popular options:

Canva

Canva is a user-friendly design platform that offers a variety of customizable templates and design elements for creating digital vision boards. Whether you prefer a sleek and modern aesthetic or a whimsical and romantic vibe, *Canva* has templates to suit every style. Choose from a wide range of images, graphics, fonts, and colors to bring your wedding vision to life. With *Canva's* intuitive interface, you can easily drag and drop elements, resize and arrange them, and add text or annotations to personalize your board.

Loverly

Loverly is a wedding planning app that allows you to save your favorite wedding ideas and build event mood boards. Browse through thousands of curated images, articles, and vendor recommendations to discover inspiration for every aspect of your wedding. With *Loverly's* intuitive interface, you can create custom mood boards by selecting and arranging images that resonate with your vision. Share your boards with your partner, wedding planner, or vendors to collaborate and communicate your ideas effectively.

Wepik

Wepik is an online design tool that provides free wedding vision board templates to edit and personalize. Choose from a selection of professionally designed templates featuring stunning imagery and customizable elements. Whether you're planning a classic wedding, a bohemian celebration, or a destination getaway, Wepik has templates to suit your style. Customize your board by adding your images, text, and graphics, and then download or share it with others to gather feedback and inspiration.

Remember, your dream board is a living document that evolves as your wedding planning progresses. Have fun with it and let it truly represent your and your partner's aspirations for your big day!

Cultural and Family Traditions

Integrating cultural and family traditions into your wedding is a heartfelt way to honor your heritage and create a ceremony that's uniquely yours. These traditions can add depth and meaning to your celebration, connecting you and your guests to your cultural roots and family history. Here's a guide to help you incorporate these elements into your special day:

Talk to Family Members

Engaging with family members is an essential first step in discovering and understanding cherished traditions or stories. Here's how to start:

1. **Ask open-ended questions:** Use questions that delve into their memories of weddings and cultural celebrations. For example, "What were some of the most memorable traditions at your wedding?" or "Can you share any special rituals that have been passed down in our family?"

2. **Record their stories:** Take notes or record these conversations to capture the details accurately. This can also be a wonderful keepsake to share with future generations.

3. **Seek advice and guidance:** Family members often have valuable insights and suggestions for incorporating traditions into your wedding. Ask for their advice on how to adapt these rituals to fit your wedding style and personal preferences.

Blending Traditions

Combining traditions from both partners' backgrounds can create a rich and diverse wedding experience. Here are some ideas:

- **Dual ceremonies:** If you and your partner come from different cultural backgrounds, consider having two separate ceremonies to honor each tradition. This approach ensures that both cultures are fully represented.

- **Integrated rituals:** Find ways to blend elements from both cultures into a single ceremony. For example, you might incorporate the South African Lobola ceremony, which involves negotiating a bridal price, with the Indian Baraat procession, where the groom arrives in a joyous parade.

- **Fusion cuisine and music:** Reflect on your diverse backgrounds in your wedding menu and music. Serve dishes from both cultures and create a playlist that includes traditional songs from each side of the family.

Modern Interpretations of Old Traditions

Adapting old traditions to suit your personal style and contemporary life can make them more meaningful and relevant.

Here's how to modernize traditional elements:

- **Symbolic gift exchange:** Instead of a traditional dowry, consider a symbolic gift exchange that honors the spirit of the tradition. This could be a meaningful object or a donation to a charity that reflects your shared values.

- **Contemporary attire:** While traditional wedding attire is beautiful and significant, you can also incorporate modern touches. For instance, a bride might wear a traditional dress for the ceremony and change into a modern gown for the reception.

- **Personalized rituals:** Customize traditional rituals to reflect your unique story. For example, if handfasting is a tradition in your culture, choose ribbons or cords that have special significance to you and your partner.

Incorporating cultural and family traditions into your wedding not only honors your heritage but also enriches your ceremony with meaning and significance. Here are some additional tips to make these traditions a seamless part of your celebration:

- **Educate your guests:** Provide explanations of the traditions in your wedding program or through announcements. This helps guests understand and appreciate the significance of each ritual.

- **Involve family members:** Invite family members to participate in traditional rituals. This not only honors them but also adds a personal touch to your ceremony.

- **Stay true to yourselves:** While it's important to honor traditions, ensure that your wedding reflects who you are as a couple. Choose and adapt traditions that resonate with you and make your day uniquely yours.

By thoughtfully incorporating cultural and family traditions into your wedding, you create a rich tapestry of experiences that celebrate your past while looking forward to your future together. Let these traditions add depth, meaning, and a personal touch to your special day, making it a truly one-of-a-kind celebration.

Wedding Themes and Styles

Choosing a wedding theme that resonates with your style is an exciting journey that sets the tone for your special day. Here are some examples to help you navigate through the process and find the perfect theme for your wedding:

Rustic

Ideal for nature lovers, a rustic theme embraces the beauty of the outdoors with natural textures like wood, burlap, and wildflowers. Think charming barn venues, cozy string lights, and DIY touches that create a warm and inviting atmosphere.

Modern

Sleek lines, minimalist decor, and a monochrome palette characterize the modern theme. Embrace contemporary elegance with clean, geometric shapes, and chic metallic accents. Keep the focus on simplicity and sophistication for a timeless and sophisticated wedding.

Boho

Free-spirited and eclectic, the boho theme celebrates individuality with earthy elements, vibrant colors, and vintage accessories. Create a relaxed and whimsical vibe with dreamcatchers, macramé details, and flowing fabrics that capture the essence of bohemian style.

Vintage

A nod to the past, the vintage theme exudes timeless elegance with antique details and classic touches. Embrace retro charm with lace, pearls, and heirloom accents that evoke the romance of bygone eras. Vintage-inspired venues and attire complete the old-world allure.

Glam

For those who love opulence and grandeur, the glam theme is the epitome of luxury. Think glittering decor, lavish floral arrangements, and sumptuous fabrics that exude sophistication and style. Create a glamorous ambiance with sparkling chandeliers, mirrored accents, and extravagant centerpieces.

Maintaining Thematic Consistency

To ensure a cohesive and memorable wedding experience, maintain consistency throughout your chosen theme:

- **Attire:** Choose dresses, suits, and accessories that reflect the style and mood of your theme, whether it's rustic chic or modern elegance.

- **Decor:** From centerpieces to lighting, ensure all decor elements complement each other and contribute to the overall ambiance of your wedding.

- **Invitations:** Set the tone for your wedding with invitations that give guests a glimpse of the style and theme they can expect on your special day.

- **Menu:** Even your food and drink offerings can echo your theme, with signature cocktails, themed appetizers, and desserts that reflect the aesthetic of your wedding.

Personalizing Popular Themes

Make your wedding theme truly unique by infusing personal touches and elements that reflect your love story:

- **Symbols:** Integrate personal symbols, like a family crest or a shared hobby, into your decor to add meaning and significance.

- **Story elements:** Weave in aspects of your favorite love story or fairy tale to create a narrative that is uniquely yours and captures the essence of your relationship.

Remember, your wedding theme should be a reflection of who you are as a couple. It's not just about aesthetics; it's about telling your story and creating an atmosphere that feels like home. With careful planning and thoughtful consideration, you can create a wedding that is as beautiful and unique as your love for each other.

The Significance of Color Schemes

Choosing the right color scheme for your wedding is a significant decision that sets the tone, atmosphere, and overall aesthetic of your special day. Here's a guide to help you select a palette that resonates with you and creates the perfect backdrop for your celebration:

Emotional Impact

Colors have the remarkable ability to evoke specific emotions and create a particular ambiance:

- **Warm tones:** Reds and oranges can generate a warm, energetic atmosphere, perfect for adding a vibrant and passionate feel to your wedding.

- **Cool tones:** Blues and greens often create a calming effect, ideal for weddings that aim to evoke tranquility and serenity.

Visual Harmony

A well-chosen color scheme can bring visual harmony to your wedding, making it aesthetically pleasing and photographically beautiful. When selecting colors, consider how they complement each other and work together to create a cohesive and unified look throughout your wedding décor and attire.

Color Psychology

Different colors can influence mood and perception, allowing you to set the desired tone for your wedding:

- **Tranquility and stability:** Blues are associated with tranquility and stability, making them an excellent choice for creating a serene and peaceful ambiance.

- **Passion and excitement:** Reds are linked to passion and excitement, adding a bold and vibrant touch to your wedding atmosphere.

Seasonal Color Choices

Consider the season in which your wedding takes place when selecting your color palette:

- **Spring:** Opt for pastel shades like blush pink or baby blue, which reflect the season's fresh and blooming nature.

- **Summer:** Bright and cheerful colors like sunshine yellow or sky blue work well for summer weddings, capturing the warmth and joy of the season.

- **Fall:** Rich, earthy tones such as burnt orange and deep burgundy complement the autumnal backdrop, adding warmth and depth to your wedding décor.

- **Winter:** Icy colors like silver and pale blue, paired with white, can create a winter wonderland theme, capturing the magic and elegance of the season.

Coordinating Colors With the Wedding Party

Ensure that the colors you choose for your wedding décor complement the attire of your wedding party:

- **Bridal party attire:** Match the bridesmaids' dresses and groomsmen's ties to the wedding color palette for a cohesive and unified look.

- **Complementary outfits:** Choose attire for the wedding party that complements the decor and overall aesthetic of your wedding. For example, if your colors are navy and gold, bridesmaids could wear navy dresses with gold accessories, and groomsmen could sport navy suits with gold ties.

The colors you choose for your wedding should not only be beautiful but also meaningful to you and your partner. They should reflect your personalities, style, and the feelings you want to share with your guests on your wedding day. Take your time exploring different color options and selecting a palette that resonates with your vision and creates a memorable and enchanting experience for everyone involved.

Chapter 2:

Budgeting and Financing Your Wedding

At the heart of your wedding planning journey is the art of budget mastery. While dreaming about your perfect day is exhilarating, the financial aspect can often feel daunting. This chapter empowers you with expert tips and tools, helping you to splurge wisely and save smartly, ensuring your dream wedding is financially achievable.

Establishing a Budget Framework

Creating a budget framework is the foundation of a successful wedding planning process. Here's how to establish a budget that will keep you on track and ensure your special day is everything you dreamed of without financial stress.

Step-by-Step Budget Framework

1. **Determine your total budget:** Assess your savings, family contributions, and any other financial resources. Establish a clear total budget amount.

2. **Prioritize your spending:** Identify the most critical aspects of your wedding, such as venue, catering, and photography. Allocate funds to these high-priority items first. Then, distribute the remaining funds to other elements like attire, entertainment, and decor.

3. **Keep detailed records:** Maintain a detailed and up-to-date record of all expenses. Use budgeting tools, spreadsheets, or apps to track every penny.

4. **Assess and allocate funds:** Confirm your total budget, considering all funding sources. Divide your budget into key categories, prioritizing funds for essential elements.

5. **Implement Flexible Budgeting:** Allocate 5-10% of your budget for unforeseen expenses. Allow flexibility in less critical categories to accommodate changes.

6. **Regularly Review and Adjust:** Schedule regular budget check-ins to compare planned versus actual expenses. Be ready to shift funds if some areas cost more or less than expected.

Remember, flexibility and regular review are keys to a successful wedding budget. With a well-planned budget, you can confidently navigate your wedding planning journey, ensuring your special day is both memorable and financially manageable.

Cost-Saving Tips for Big-Ticket Items

Planning a wedding involves managing significant expenses, especially for key elements like the venue, catering, and photography. Here are some practical strategies to help you save money on these big-ticket items, allowing you to allocate your budget more effectively and potentially add special touches to your day.

Implementing Cost-Saving Strategies

1. **Off-peak discounts:** Identify the off-peak times for your chosen venue and vendors. Ask for discounts for booking during these periods. Vendors may be more flexible and willing to offer better deals.

2. **Package deals:** Contact vendors to inquire about package deals that might bundle multiple services at a lower rate. Evaluate different package deals to find the best value for your needs.

3. **Catering choices:** Discuss buffet options with your caterer to understand the cost savings compared to plated service. Work with your caterer to create a menu featuring local, seasonal ingredients. This can add a unique, local touch to your wedding while saving money. Consider a streamlined menu with fewer high-quality choices to keep costs down without sacrificing taste or style.

Additional Tips for Cost Management

- **Early bookings:** Booking key services well in advance can lock in current rates and avoid potential price increases.

- **DIY elements:** Incorporate DIY projects where feasible, such as creating your own centerpieces or wedding favors.

- **Vendor negotiations:** Don't hesitate to negotiate with vendors. Many are open to customizing packages to fit your budget.

- **Review contracts carefully:** Ensure you understand all terms and conditions in vendor contracts to avoid unexpected costs.

Careful planning and smart negotiations can make your dream wedding both memorable and affordable, leaving room for those extra touches that make your day uniquely yours.

Understanding Wedding Costs

A wedding requires careful financial planning and a clear understanding of the costs involved. Typical wedding expenses are divided into several categories. Here's a general guideline on how to allocate your total budget:

Expense Type	Percentage
Venue and catering: This includes the cost of renting the venue, food, and beverages	40-50%
Photography and videography: Capturing your big day through professional photos and videos.	10-15%
Attire and beauty: Wedding dress, groom's attire, hair, makeup, and other beauty treatments.	5-10%
Music/entertainment: Live bands, DJs, and other forms of entertainment.	10%
Flowers and decor: Floral arrangements, centerpieces, lighting, and other decor elements.	10%
Favors and gifts: Gifts for guests, bridal parties, and any additional favors.	2-3%
Transportation: Wedding day transportation for the couple and possibly the bridal party.	2-3%

Hidden Costs

Wedding budgets often overlook certain costs that can add up. Here are some common hidden fees to watch out for:

- **Service fees:** Additional fees like cake cutting and corkage.
- **Gratuities:** Tips for vendors such as DJs, musicians, and waitstaff.
- **Setup/breakdown charges:** Extra costs for setting up and taking down event decor.
- **Trial services:** Costs for hair and makeup trials, menu tastings, and other pre-wedding services are not always included in initial quotes.

The location of your wedding also significantly impacts costs. Urban areas and popular destinations generally have higher venue and vendor costs than rural settings. And peak wedding seasons, such as spring and summer, typically command higher prices for venues and services due to high demand.

Practical Steps for Budgeting

Creating a realistic and effective budget is essential for managing wedding expenses and ensuring your special day is both memorable and financially manageable. Here are some practical steps to help you navigate the budgeting process:

Research Specific Costs

1. **Investigate costs:** Research the costs of venues, vendors, and other services in your chosen location. Request quotes and compare the pricing of different vendors to find the best value.
2. **Compare prices by location:** Consider the cost differences between urban and rural areas. If you have flexibility in your wedding location, this comparison can help you choose a more budget-friendly option without compromising on quality.

Account for Hidden Fees

1. **Ask about additional charges:** When meeting with vendors, always inquire about potential hidden fees such as service charges, overtime fees, or setup/breakdown costs.
2. **Include a buffer:** Allocate a contingency fund in your budget, typically 5-10% of your total budget, to cover unexpected expenses and last-minute changes.

Consider Off-Peak Discounts

1. **Book during off-peak times:** Schedule your wedding during off-peak seasons or weekdays to take advantage of lower rates. Off-peak weddings often have reduced prices for venues and vendors, providing significant savings.

2. **Negotiate for discounts:** Some vendors might be open to negotiating discounts or offering package deals if you book their services during less busy times.

Regular Budget Reviews

1. **Periodic reviews:** Regularly review your budget to ensure you stay within your planned expenses. Compare your budget estimates against actual costs and make adjustments as needed.

2. **Adjust allocations:** Be prepared to reallocate funds if certain elements of your wedding end up costing more or less than anticipated. Flexibility in your budget allows you to accommodate unexpected changes without financial stress.

Detailed Record-Keeping

1. **Maintain detailed records:** Keep a comprehensive record of all wedding-related expenses. Document payments, receipts, and any changes to your budget to stay organized.

2. **Use budgeting tools:** Utilize budgeting tools or apps designed for wedding planning to track your spending and manage your budget efficiently. These tools can help you stay on top of your expenses and provide a clear overview of your financial progress.

By understanding the typical wedding cost and being mindful of potential hidden fees, you can create a realistic and effective budget. This approach allows you to manage your finances better and make informed decisions, ensuring your special day is both memorable and financially manageable. Remember, thorough research, regular budget reviews, and detailed record-keeping are key to avoiding surprises and keeping your wedding planning on track.

Planning a wedding involves balancing dreams with practical considerations. By following these steps, you can achieve a beautiful wedding that reflects your style and stays within your financial means.

DIY Versus Professional Services: Making Informed Decisions for Your Wedding

Deciding between DIY and professional services for your wedding is a significant choice that affects your budget and your event's quality. Here's a comprehensive guide to help you navigate this decision:

DIY Approach

Deciding to take the DIY route for your wedding can lead to significant savings and personal touches that make your day uniquely yours. However, it also requires careful consideration of time, skills, and potential stress. Here's an in-depth look at the DIY approach to wedding planning:

Cost-Effective Benefits

DIY projects can substantially reduce expenses. For instance, making your own centerpieces or invitations can be much cheaper than purchasing them. By saving on certain elements, you can redirect funds to other high-priority areas like the venue or catering, enhancing overall quality without breaking the bank.

With the money saved through DIY, you have more financial flexibility. This allows you to splurge on essential elements that matter most to you and your partner, such as a designer dress or a gourmet menu.

Time-Consuming Aspects

DIY projects require a significant time investment. This includes researching ideas, gathering materials, and crafting or building items. Successful DIY requires meticulous time management to complete all projects before the wedding day.

As the wedding day approaches, the pressure to complete DIY projects can become overwhelming, especially if you encounter unexpected issues. Juggling multiple DIY tasks alongside other wedding planning duties can lead to burnout if not carefully managed.

Skill Requirement

Evaluate your skills honestly. If you or your network lack experience in areas like crafting, design, or construction, some DIY projects might be too challenging. While DIY can be a fun opportunity to learn new skills, consider whether you have the time and resources to develop these skills adequately before your wedding.

The quality of DIY projects depends heavily on the skill and precision of the person executing them. Simple mistakes can affect the outcome. Practice makes perfect. If you decide to DIY, ensure you have ample time for trial and error, and don't rush the process.

Practical Tips for DIY Success

1. **Start early:** Begin planning and executing DIY projects as early as possible. This reduces last-minute stress and allows time for adjustments if needed.

2. **Create a timeline:** Develop a detailed timeline for each project. Break down tasks into manageable steps and set realistic deadlines to stay on track.

3. **Get organized:** Keep all materials and tools organized to streamline the DIY process. Designate a specific workspace to avoid clutter and confusion.

4. **Enlist help:** Don't be afraid to ask for help from friends and family. Organize DIY parties where you can work on projects together, making the process more enjoyable and efficient.

5. **Know when to delegate:** Recognize your limits. For complex or critical elements, it might be worth hiring a professional to ensure quality and reduce stress.

6. **Set a budget:** Even for DIY projects, set a budget to avoid overspending on materials and tools. Track all expenses to stay within your financial plan.

While DIY can save money and add personal touches, blending DIY with professional services can offer the best of both worlds. For example:

- **DIY Invitations and Favors:** Add a personal touch with handmade invitations and favors.

- **Professional Photography and Catering:** Ensure critical elements like photography and catering are handled by professionals to guarantee quality and reliability.

The DIY approach to wedding planning can be rewarding both financially and creatively. By saving money, managing your time wisely, and leveraging your skills, you can personalize your wedding to reflect your unique style. However, it's essential to balance DIY projects with professional help where needed to ensure a smooth and stress-free wedding day. With careful planning and a realistic assessment of your abilities, you can make your dream wedding a beautiful reality.

Professional Services

When planning your wedding, opting for professional services can offer a range of benefits that ensure your big day is seamless, beautiful, and memorable. Here's an in-depth look at the advantages of hiring professionals for your wedding:

Higher Costs

Hiring professionals can be costly, often requiring a significant portion of your budget. Services like photography, catering, and event planning typically come at a premium.

Despite the higher costs, professional services often deliver exceptional value. The expertise, efficiency, and high-quality results professionals provide can justify the investment, ensuring your wedding meets your highest expectations.

Time-Saving Benefits

Professionals manage the intricate details of your wedding, from vendor coordination to timeline execution. This saves you considerable time that can be better spent on personal touches and enjoying the planning process.

By delegating key tasks to professionals, you can focus on other important aspects of your wedding, such as spending time with loved ones or perfecting your vows.

Knowing that experienced vendors are in charge of critical elements can significantly reduce your stress levels. Professionals are adept at handling unexpected issues, ensuring that your wedding day proceeds smoothly. The reliability and expertise of professional services provide peace of mind, allowing you to enjoy your engagement period without the constant worry of managing every detail.

Expertise and Reliability

Professionals bring a wealth of experience and specialized skills to your wedding. Their expertise ensures that every element, from photography to floral arrangements, is executed to the highest standard. Professional vendors use top-of-the-line equipment and materials, contributing to the overall quality and aesthetic of your wedding.

Most professional services include contracts that outline the scope of work, deadlines, and payment terms. These legal agreements provide clarity and protection, ensuring that both parties are on the same page.

Many professionals offer guarantees on their services, assuring that they will meet your expectations. If issues arise, these guarantees often include provisions for rectifying problems, adding an extra layer of security to your planning process.

Practical Steps for Choosing Professional Services

1. **Research and reviews:** Look for reputable professionals with positive reviews and a strong portfolio. Personal recommendations from friends or family can also be invaluable.

2. **Interview multiple vendors:** Meet with several vendors to discuss your vision and get a sense of their style, approach, and personality. This helps ensure a good fit for your wedding.

3. **Request detailed quotes:** Obtain detailed quotes from potential vendors, including a breakdown of all costs. This helps you compare services and make informed decisions within your budget.

4. **Check contracts thoroughly:** Review contracts carefully before signing. Ensure all details, including services, costs, deadlines, and cancellation policies, are clearly outlined.

5. **Communicate expectations:** Clearly communicate your expectations and vision to your vendors. Provide examples and discuss any specific requirements or concerns to ensure alignment.

While hiring professional services for your wedding involves higher costs, the benefits in terms of time savings, reduced stress, and guaranteed quality make it a worthwhile investment. Professionals bring expertise, high-quality equipment, and reliability, ensuring your wedding day is executed flawlessly. By thoroughly researching, interviewing, and clearly communicating with your chosen vendors, you can create a wedding that exceeds your expectations, allowing you to enjoy every moment of your special day.

Deciding Between DIY and Professional Services: A Balanced Approach

Choosing between DIY and professional services is a critical decision in wedding planning that can significantly impact your budget, the quality of your wedding, and the overall planning experience. Here's a comprehensive guide to help you make the best choices for your special day:

Identify Priorities

Sit down with your partner and identify the most important aspects of your wedding. This could be the venue, photography, catering, or entertainment.

Allocate a larger portion of your budget to these high-priority areas. Ensuring these elements are top-notch can enhance the overall experience of your wedding.

Assess Skills

Honestly assess your skills and those of friends or family members willing to help. Consider your proficiency in areas like crafting, design, and event planning.

Factor in the time and effort required for DIY projects. Ensure you have enough time to complete these tasks without adding undue stress as the wedding day approaches.

Budget Analysis

Calculate the potential savings from doing projects yourself. This could include making your own invitations, centerpieces, or favors.

Weigh the savings against the value of professional services. Consider how much time and stress you'll save by hiring experts who can deliver high-quality results efficiently.

Hybrid Approach

Consider a hybrid approach, blending DIY and professional services to balance cost and quality. For example:

- **DIY projects:** Invitations, favors, and simple decor items can often be managed with a personal touch, adding charm and personalization without significant cost.

- **Professional services:** Hire professionals for critical elements like photography, catering, and floral arrangements to handle these essential aspects expertly.

Play to your strengths by choosing DIY projects that match your abilities and leaving more complex tasks to professionals.

Practical Steps to Implement Your Decision

1. **Make a list:** Create a detailed list of all wedding tasks and categorize them as DIY, professional, or hybrid.

2. **Set realistic deadlines:** Establish timelines for DIY projects to ensure they are completed well before the wedding date, allowing time for adjustments if needed.

3. **Budget allocation:** Clearly define your budget for each category. Allocate more funds to professional services in high-priority areas and set a budget limit for DIY projects to avoid overspending.

4. **Resource check:** Ensure you have all the necessary materials and tools for DIY projects. Consider borrowing or renting equipment to save on costs.

5. **Seek help:** Don't hesitate to ask for help from friends and family. Many people are eager to contribute to your special day and can offer valuable skills and support.

6. **Trial runs:** Conduct trial runs for DIY projects to refine your process and ensure the final product meets your expectations. This is especially important for elements like decorations or homemade desserts.

Balancing DIY and professional services requires thoughtful consideration of your budget, the importance of quality in specific areas, and the resources available. By identifying your priorities, assessing your skills, conducting a thorough budget analysis, and considering a hybrid approach, you can create a wedding that reflects your unique vision and stays within your budget. This balanced strategy ensures high-quality results where they matter most and allows for personal touches that make your wedding truly special.

Ultimately, the goal is to create a memorable and stress-free day for you and your guests. By carefully considering the time, cost, quality, and resource availability, you can make informed decisions that align with your vision and budget. Whether you choose DIY projects, professional services, or a combination of both, the key is to plan thoughtfully and enjoy the process of bringing your dream wedding to life.

Chapter 3:

Organizing the Details

Now, let's dive into the intricate and exciting world of wedding planning details. This chapter is your comprehensive guide to navigating the essential elements to bring your wedding vision to life. From selecting the perfect venue to choosing top-notch vendors, I'll help you ensure every detail aligns seamlessly with your dream day. Let's start making your wedding planning journey as smooth and enjoyable as possible!

Venue Selection Criteria

Selecting the perfect venue is an important step in wedding planning, as it sets the stage for your entire celebration. You want to consider three main factors before choosing the perfect spot.

1. **Size:** Ensure the venue can comfortably accommodate your guest list and any additional activities you plan, such as a dance floor or photo booth. Ask about maximum capacities for different setups (e.g., seated dinner, cocktail reception).

2. **Location:** Consider the venue's proximity to major transportation hubs like airports and train stations. Check for adequate parking or shuttle services for guests who will be driving. Ensure the venue is easily accessible for all guests, including those with mobility challenges.

3. **Style compatibility:** The venue should naturally complement your wedding theme, whether it's rustic, modern, classic, or bohemian. Look for architectural styles and interior designs that enhance your vision.

Visiting venues in person gives you a true sense of the space, lighting, and overall ambiance. Photos can be misleading, so first-hand experience is invaluable. Pay attention to the layout and how it will work with your event. Consider the flow of guests from the ceremony to the reception, and identify any potential bottlenecks or awkward spaces.

Discuss your vision with the venue managers. They can provide insights into how previous events were set up and offer suggestions to maximize the space. Understand any limitations or unique features that might impact your plans.

Choose a venue whose architecture aligns with your theme. For instance, a historic mansion might be perfect for a vintage wedding, while a sleek, modern loft would suit a contemporary affair. Look for existing decor elements that match your aesthetic, such as chandeliers, wall colors, and flooring. This can save on decorating costs and effort. Consider how the venue's gardens, terraces, or views contribute to your theme. Outdoor areas can be particularly impactful for ceremonies, cocktail hours, or photo opportunities.

Contracts and Negotiations

The next step is to ensure you understand all the terms of the contract and negotiate terms that meet your needs. Here are some key aspects to consider:

Terms and Fees

- **Cancellation policy:** Thoroughly review the venue's cancellation policies. Understanding the conditions under which you can cancel the booking and any associated fees or penalties.

- **Refunds and deadlines:** Note the deadlines for cancellations to avoid hefty penalties and check if you're eligible for partial or full refunds under certain conditions.

Payment Schedule

- **Deposit amount:** Know the deposit required to secure the venue. This is typically a percentage of the total cost and is often non-refundable.

- **Payment milestones:** Understand the full payment schedule, including any interim payments leading up to the wedding. This helps with managing your budget and planning financial commitments effectively.

What's Included

- **Venue package:** Clarify the amenities and services included in the venue hire. Common inclusions might be tables, chairs, linens, AV equipment, and basic staffing.

- **Extra costs:** Identify any additional items or services that might incur extra costs. For example, you might need to rent specialty chairs, additional lighting, or sound systems if they're not included.

Rules and Limitations

- **Noise ordinances and curfews:** Some venues have strict noise ordinances or curfews, particularly in residential areas. Ensure that your event can accommodate these rules without disrupting your plans.

- **Preferred vendors:** Some venues have preferred or exclusive vendor lists, meaning you may be required to use their caterers, florists, or other service providers. This can impact both your budget and your vision for the wedding.

- **Decoration policies:** Understand any restrictions on decorations, such as the use of candles, hanging items from ceilings, or the type of materials allowed. These rules are often in place to protect the property and ensure safety.

- **Catering and alcohol policies:** Verify any specific policies regarding catering and alcohol service. Some venues might restrict outside caterers or require licensed bartenders to serve alcohol.

Tips for Successful Negotiations

1. **Be prepared:** Before entering negotiations, clearly understand your budget and priorities. Know what you're willing to compromise on and what is non-negotiable.

2. **Ask questions:** Don't hesitate to ask for clarification on any unclear terms and conditions. It's better to address any uncertainties upfront rather than face unexpected issues later.

3. **Get everything in writing:** Ensure all agreements and changes are documented in the contract. Verbal agreements should be confirmed in writing to avoid misunderstandings.

4. **Negotiate inclusions:** If the venue doesn't include certain amenities you need, ask if they can be added at no extra cost or for a reduced fee. Venues may be flexible, especially during off-peak seasons.

5. **Read the fine print:** Carefully review all terms and conditions in the contract, including any clauses related to liability, insurance, and the venue's responsibilities.

Some other tips that you can keep in mind are:

- **Compare and contrast:** Make a list of pros and cons for each venue you visit. Compare them based on your criteria and budget.

- **Flexibility:** Be open to considering different dates or times if it means securing your dream venue at a better rate.

- **Thorough inspection:** Don't be afraid to ask for a detailed tour, including backstage areas, storage spaces, and any on-site accommodations.

By understanding these key elements of venue contracts and being proactive in negotiations, you can secure a venue that fits your vision and budget while avoiding potential pitfalls. Remember, a well-negotiated contract sets the foundation for a smooth and enjoyable wedding planning process.

Vetting and Selecting Vendors

Choosing the right vendors is crucial to ensuring your wedding day is everything you've dreamed of. The right vendors will not only deliver top-notch services but will also work harmoniously to bring your vision to life.

Portfolio and References

Examine the past work of potential vendors to gauge their style, quality, and professionalism. For photographers and florists, a portfolio can show their ability to capture and create beautiful moments and settings that align with their vision.

Look for various examples in their portfolio to ensure they can handle different settings, lighting, and themes. This can give you confidence in their adaptability and creativity.

Request references or testimonials from past clients. This provides insight into the vendor's reliability, punctuality, and how well they meet their clients' expectations.

Check online reviews on platforms like WeddingWire, The Knot, or Yelp. Consistent positive feedback is a good indicator of a vendor's reliability and quality.

Matching Vendors to Vision

Ensure that vendors involved in creative aspects, such as photographers, florists, and bakers, can match or adapt their style to suit your wedding theme. Look for those who have successfully executed similar themes in the past.

During initial meetings, discuss your vision and ask for their input. Vendors who bring innovative ideas and show enthusiasm for your theme are often the best fit.

Have in-depth discussions with your vendors about your wedding vision. Provide mood boards, color schemes, and specific examples to ensure they understand and can execute your ideas.

For services like hair, makeup, and catering, schedule trial runs or tastings to see firsthand if their work aligns with your expectations.

Communication and Flexibility

Establish clear and consistent communication channels with your vendors. Regular updates and check-ins help ensure everyone is on the same page and progress is tracked.

Designate a primary contact person (yourself or a wedding planner) to streamline communications and avoid misunderstandings.

Assess the vendor's willingness to accommodate changes or last-minute requests. This flexibility is crucial for handling any unforeseen circumstances that may arise during the planning process.

Discuss potential contingency plans for common issues (like weather problems for outdoor events) to ensure the vendor is prepared to adapt smoothly.

The key to a successful vendor relationship is mutual understanding, clear communication, and flexibility. This careful selection process will create a smooth, enjoyable, and memorable wedding day.

Guest List Management

Managing your wedding guest list and seating arrangements can be streamlined with the right strategies and tools. Start by dividing your guest:

- Begin by listing immediate family members and close friends. These are the people you cannot imagine your special day without. Their presence is paramount to your celebration.

- Next, include extended relatives, friends, colleagues, and acquaintances. This helps you prioritize who should be there based on the strength of your relationship and your day-to-day interactions.

- Establish a maximum number of guests early in the process to avoid over-inviting. This helps in maintaining your budget and adhering to venue capacity constraints. Knowing your limit upfront makes it easier to decide who to invite.

Once you have your list and the invites have been sent, you can use digital tools like The Knot's guest list manager or similar apps to track RSVPs. These tools can update your list in real time, helping you keep an accurate headcount and manage invitations and responses seamlessly.

What's great about these apps is that you can set up automated reminders for guests who haven't responded. This ensures you get timely responses and can finalize your guest count without last-minute surprises.

Seating Arrangements

Managing the seating arrangements is one of the key components that significantly impact your guest's experience. Let's take a look at some strategies you can use to streamline the process.

Digital Tools for Efficiency

Use the seating chart tools available in guest management apps to easily create and adjust the seating plans. These tools allow you to visualize the layout, making placing guests in suitable locations easier and ensuring everyone has a good view of the proceedings.

These tools provide flexibility to move guests around and see the impact of each change in real-time. This helps you experiment with different configurations until you find the perfect arrangement.

Grouping Guests Thoughtfully

Arrange seating to encourage conversation among guests who will enjoy each other's company. Group friends with shared interests, backgrounds, or histories together to enhance their experience and ensure lively discussions. Place guests who might not know many people at the wedding with outgoing and friendly individuals. This can help them feel more comfortable and included.

Mixing Different Groups

Consider blending different groups, such as family members and friends, to foster new connections. For example, mix your college friends with your partner's childhood friends to create a diverse and engaging atmosphere. Designate specific tables for VIP guests, such as immediate family or the bridal party, to ensure they have a central and significant place in the seating arrangement.

Mindful of Relationships

Be mindful of relationships and potential conflicts when creating your seating chart. Keep guests with known disagreements or uncomfortable histories apart to avoid any tension during the celebration.

Ensure that important guests, such as elderly family members or those with mobility issues, are seated near key locations like the restrooms or exits for their convenience.

Communication and Feedback

Don't hesitate to seek input from close family members or friends about seating arrangements. They might have insights into dynamics you are unaware of, helping you make more informed decisions.

Have a backup plan for any last-minute changes. Unexpected guests or cancellations can occur, so being prepared with alternative seating options can save time and reduce stress.

Table Numbers and Place Cards

Use clear and creative table numbers or names to help guests find their seats easily. Place cards can add a personal touch and help guests feel special. Incorporate decorative elements that match your wedding theme to enhance the aesthetic appeal of the seating arrangements. This adds to the overall ambiance and guest experience.

Navigating Plus-Ones and Family Dynamics

Establish clear criteria for plus-ones to maintain control over your guest list size and dynamics. For instance, consider only allowing plus-ones for guests in long-term relationships or traveling from afar.

Communicate openly with family members about guest list limitations. Seek compromises where necessary, ensuring everyone understands the reasons behind your decisions.

By implementing these strategies and utilizing digital tools, you can streamline the process of managing your wedding guest list and seating arrangements. This organized approach helps you focus on creating a memorable and enjoyable experience for you and your guests.

Ceremony Planning

Planning your wedding ceremony with meticulous attention to detail ensures a memorable and smooth-running event.

Typically, a wedding ceremony follows this sequence:

1. **Processional:** The entrance of the wedding party and the couple.
2. **Welcome speech:** A greeting by the officiant to welcome guests.
3. **Readings:** Selected passages, poems, or religious texts read by chosen individuals.
4. **Exchange of vows:** The couple's personal promises to each other.
5. **Ring exchange:** The giving and receiving of rings as a symbol of their commitment.
6. **Pronouncement of marriage:** The officiant declares the couple married.
7. **Recessional:** The exit of the couple and the wedding party.

Assign clear roles to your wedding party and family members:

1. **Best man:** Responsible for holding the rings and assisting the groom.
2. **Maid of honor:** Helps the bride with her dress and bouquet.
3. **Bridesmaids and groomsmen:** Support the couple and participate in the processional and recessional.
4. **Readers:** Chosen individuals to perform readings.
5. **Ushers:** Assist guests with seating.

Clearly communicate each person's role and responsibilities well before the wedding day to avoid any confusion. Conduct a rehearsal to ensure everyone understands their part in the ceremony. This helps with timing and placement and addresses any last-minute concerns.

Timing and Flow of the Ceremony

Crafting a well-timed and seamlessly flowing ceremony is essential to making your special day both memorable and enjoyable for everyone involved. Here's how to ensure everything unfolds smoothly:

- **Comprehensive planning:** Develop a detailed ceremony timeline, specifying how long each segment should last. This helps maintain a smooth flow and ensures no part of the ceremony feels rushed or excessively prolonged.

- **Balanced segments:** Allocate appropriate time for each part of the ceremony, such as the processional, readings, vows, ring exchange, and recessional. This balance prevents the event from dragging or feeling hurried.

- **Precision:** Time each segment precisely to fit within the overall ceremony duration. Consider practice runs to refine the timing and make adjustments as needed.

- **Allowances for transitions:** Include buffer times for transitions between segments to accommodate any unexpected delays and maintain a relaxed pace.

- **Clear instructions:** Ensure that all participants, including the wedding party, officiant, and musicians, know their cues for when to walk, stand, speak, or perform their duties.

- **Rehearsal:** Conduct a rehearsal to practice and confirm that everyone understands their roles and cues, reducing the risk of mistakes on the day.

- **Music timing:** Coordinate with musicians or the DJ to cue music precisely for key moments like the processional, readings, vows, and recessional. The right music at the right time enhances the emotional impact of each segment.

- **Seamless transitions:** Ensure smooth transitions between songs or musical pieces to avoid awkward pauses or overlaps.

- **Alternative arrangements:** If you're planning an outdoor ceremony, have a plan for inclement weather, such as a tent or an alternative indoor venue. This ensures that your ceremony can proceed smoothly regardless of the weather.

- **Early decisions:** Make decisions about moving the ceremony indoors early enough to inform all guests and vendors, avoiding last-minute confusion.

- **Vendor notification:** Inform all vendors and key participants of the backup plan in advance to ensure seamless coordination if changes are necessary.

- **Guest awareness:** Communicate the backup plan to guests through your wedding website or a pre-ceremony email so they know what to expect in case of weather-related changes.

- **Written guides:** Provide vendors with detailed instructions and timelines to ensure everyone is on the same page.

- **Confirmation:** Confirm that all vendors understand the schedule and their roles well before the ceremony day.

- **Key contacts:** Share contact information for key individuals, such as the wedding planner, best man, and maid of honor, to facilitate smooth communication on the event day.

- **Emergency contacts:** Have a list of emergency contacts for quick resolution of any issues that arise.

- **Unique elements:** Incorporate personal elements like unique readings, music, or rituals that reflect your relationship and values. This makes the ceremony more meaningful and memorable for you and your guests.

- **Symbolic acts:** Consider symbolic acts like unity ceremonies (e.g., sand blending and candle lighting) to personalize your wedding further.

- **Programs:** Provide programs that outline the ceremony's order of events, helping guests follow along and know what to expect.

- **Comfort measures:** Offer water, fans, or heaters for outdoor ceremonies to keep guests comfortable. Ensure accessible seating for elderly or disabled guests to accommodate everyone's needs.

- **Personalized ceremony:** Work closely with your officiant to craft a ceremony that reflects your personality and beliefs, ensuring it feels personalized and meaningful.

- **Flow and pacing:** Discuss the flow and pacing of the ceremony with your officiant to ensure it aligns with your vision and maintains a good rhythm.

By following these guidelines, you'll be well-prepared to manage the intricacies of your wedding ceremony, ensuring it is a joyous occasion for you and your guests. Remember, the key to a successful ceremony lies in the details and thorough preparation.

Chapter 4:

Personal Touches and Memorable Experiences

This chapter will help you personalize your special day with unique touches and memorable experiences that resonate deeply with you and your guests, creating lasting impressions. From interactive activity stations that engage guests in fun and creative ways to incorporating meaningful cultural elements that honor your heritage, we'll explore various ideas to make your wedding truly one-of-a-kind. You'll learn how to craft personalized vows that reflect your journey together, design themed menus and drinks that tell your love story, and implement thoughtful seating arrangements that foster connection and comfort among your guests. By paying attention to these details and adding your flair, you'll not only enhance the overall atmosphere of your wedding but also ensure that each moment is filled with significance and joy for everyone involved.

Personalized Vows and Ceremony Rituals

Personalizing your wedding with unique touches and memorable experiences can make your special day even more meaningful by reflecting your individual personalities, values, and shared history as a couple. This approach not only enhances the event's emotional impact but also creates a deeply resonant and memorable celebration for you and your guests. By incorporating personal elements, such as custom vows, cultural rituals, and interactive activities, you can ensure that your wedding day is a true reflection of your love story, leaving a lasting impression that will be cherished by everyone in attendance for years to come.

Personalized vows are a beautiful way to make your wedding ceremony uniquely yours. By expressing your heartfelt promises and reflecting on your journey as a couple, you can create a deeply moving moment that resonates with both you and your guests. Here are some tips and ideas to help you craft and deliver personalized vows:

Vow Writing Workshops

Attend vow-writing workshops or classes that can guide you through the process of crafting meaningful and personal vows. These sessions often provide templates, examples, and prompts to help you articulate your feelings and commitments.

Utilize online resources, such as articles, videos, and vow-writing guides, to gain inspiration and structure. Websites like The Knot and WeddingWire offer valuable tips and sample vows to get you started.

Consider hiring a professional vow writer if you need additional help. These experts can work with you to create vows that perfectly capture your emotions and promises, ensuring they are eloquent and impactful. Some vow writers offer personal consultations, where they learn about your relationship and help you translate your thoughts and feelings into beautifully written vows.

Meaningful Symbols

Incorporate family heirlooms into your ceremony. For instance, using a family heirloom ring during the exchange can add a layer of sentimental value and continuity.

Include traditional garments or accessories that hold sentimental value. This could be a piece of jewelry passed down through generations or traditional attire that reflects your cultural heritage.

- **Special books:** Choose a book that has significant meaning to your relationship, such as a favorite novel or a book of poetry, to be part of your ceremony decor or backdrop.

- **Artwork:** Incorporate a piece of artwork that represents your relationship. This could be a painting, a sculpture, or even a handcrafted item with personal significance.

- **Custom unity symbols:** Create a unique unity ceremony that reflects your shared values and interests. For example, you could blend two different sands, light a unity candle, or plant a tree together, symbolizing your growing relationship.

Tips for Writing and Delivering Vows

Think about significant moments in your relationship that highlight your love and commitment. Consider the qualities you admire in your partner and the promises you want to make for your future together.

Write from the heart and be genuine. Your vows should reflect your true feelings and the unique dynamics of your relationship. Don't be afraid to show vulnerability and emotion.

Practice reading your vows aloud several times before the ceremony. This will help you become comfortable with the words and ensure a smooth delivery on the big day. Consider practicing in front of a mirror or with a trusted friend.

Aim to keep your vows concise and focused. While it's important to express your feelings, keeping your vows to a few heartfelt minutes can make them more impactful and memorable.

Ensure you and your partner are on the same page regarding the tone and length of your vows. This coordination ensures that your vows complement each other and maintain a cohesive flow during the ceremony.

By following these tips and incorporating meaningful symbols, you can create personalized vows that will make your wedding ceremony truly special and unforgettable.

Unity Ceremonies

Unity ceremonies are a beautiful way to symbolize the joining of two lives into one. These rituals can add a personal and meaningful touch to your wedding ceremony, creating a lasting memory for you and your guests. Here are some popular unity ceremony ideas, along with their symbolism and customization options:

Sand Blending

The act of combining different colored sands into a single container symbolizes the inseparable blending of your lives. Once mixed, the sands cannot be separated, representing the enduring nature of your union. The completed sand art can be displayed in your home as a beautiful, lasting memento of your wedding day.

Customization

Choose sand colors that represent each of you individually, or select hues that match your wedding theme. This can add a personal touch and enhance the visual appeal of the ceremony. Use a container that holds special meaning for you, such as a vase, a jar, or a custom-made vessel with your name and wedding date engraved on it.

Candle Lighting

Lighting a unity candle together signifies the merging of two families and creating a new family unit. This ritual typically involves lighting a large central candle from two smaller candles, which are often lit by your mothers or other family members. This ceremony can be a touching way to involve your family in the ceremony, highlighting the importance of familial support and unity.

Use candles that represent your unique heritage or family traditions. For example, you could use candles that are traditionally used in cultural ceremonies or festivals. Choose candles with scents that have special meaning to you, such as a fragrance that reminds you of a significant moment in your relationship.

Handfasting

Handfasting is an ancient ritual where the couple's hands are bound together with ribbons or cords. This symbolizes the binding of your lives and your commitment to one another. Choose ribbons or cords in colors that are significant to you, or have them embroidered with your name, wedding date, or meaningful phrases.

Tree Planting

Planting a tree together serves as a living symbol of your growing relationship and commitment. The tree represents strength, growth, and nurturing for a healthy marriage. Select a tree that holds personal significance or one that will thrive in your garden or a special location. You can also plant it in a pot to take with you if you move.

Wine Blending

In a wine blending ceremony, you each pour a different wine into a single glass, creating a new and unique blend. This symbolizes the blending of your lives and creating something new together. Choose wines that you both enjoy or that have special significance in your relationship. For example, you could use wines from a winery you visited together or from regions that are meaningful to you.

Tips for Unity Ceremonies

1. **Rehearse:** Practice the ceremony beforehand to ensure a smooth execution. This can help you feel more comfortable and confident on the big day.

2. **Timing:** Ensure the unity ceremony fits seamlessly into the overall timeline of your wedding. Coordinate with your officiant to find the best moment to include it.

3. **Add personal elements:** Incorporate personal elements or modifications that reflect your relationship and values. This could include special readings, music, or involving loved ones in the ceremony.

4. **Documenting:** Consider having a photographer or videographer capture this moment from multiple angles to create lasting memories of this special part of your ceremony.

By incorporating a unity ceremony that resonates with you and your partner, you can add a unique and meaningful touch to your wedding day, creating a memorable experience for you and your guests.

Creating Lasting Memories

Your wedding day is a celebration of your love story, and incorporating personalized touches can make it truly unforgettable for both you and your guests.

Invent a new ritual or tradition that is special to your relationship, such as a unique dance or song that holds meaning for you both. This adds a personal and intimate touch to your ceremony.

Honor your heritage by incorporating cultural elements into your ceremony. Whether it's traditional attire, customs, or rituals, infusing your cultural background adds depth and significance to the proceedings.

Engage your guests with interactive activities that invite them to be part of your celebration. Consider a guestbook quilt where each guest adds a patch or a wish tree where they can hang notes of good wishes for your future together.

Share personal messages or anecdotes about your relationship during the ceremony or speeches. This lets you express your love story and gratitude to your guests, creating a heartfelt connection.

Infuse your wedding with personalized decor that reflects your personality and style. From custom table settings to signage and wedding favors, these details add a unique and memorable flair to your celebration.

Choose entertainment that resonates with your interests and passions. Whether it's a live band playing your favorite genre of music or a performance that tells your love story, special entertainment adds a touch of magic to your wedding day.

Signature Cocktails and Menu Customization

Customizing your wedding menu and offering signature cocktails are fantastic ways to add a personal touch to your special day. Here's how you can make your wedding menu and drinks truly unique:

Seasonal and Local Ingredients

Incorporate seasonal and local ingredients into your menu and signature cocktails. Fresh, in-season produce not only enhances flavor but also supports local vendors. Using the highest-quality ingredients ensures your guests enjoy the best possible culinary experience.

Sourcing locally reduces the carbon footprint associated with transporting food over long distances. Purchasing from local farmers and suppliers helps boost the local economy and supports sustainable farming practices.

Themed Menus and Drinks

Create themed menus and drinks that reflect your journey as a couple. Consider dishes or cocktails inspired by significant moments in your relationship or named after memorable dates.

Offering unique, themed dishes and drinks can make your wedding stand out and be more memorable for your guests. Aligning your menu with your chosen themes creates a cohesive and immersive experience for your guests.

Themed menus and drinks can enhance the overall atmosphere of your wedding, making it more engaging and enjoyable.

Tasting Sessions

Participate in menu and cocktail-tasting sessions with your caterer. This allows you to refine your choices, ensure the flavors meet your expectations, and make any necessary adjustments. Tasting sessions provide an opportunity to personalize dishes to better suit your tastes and those of your guests.

Tastings help you work out any kinks ahead of time, ensuring there are no surprises on your special day. Knowing exactly what to expect can reduce stress and ensure that the food and drinks will delight your guests.

Crafting an Unforgettable Dining Experience

By thoughtfully considering these elements, you'll create an unforgettable dining experience that resonates with your unique tastes and celebrates your love story. Here are additional tips to further enhance your wedding dining experience:

1. **Engagement:** Set up interactive food stations where guests can customize their dishes, such as a taco bar, pasta station, or dessert buffet.

2. **Variety:** Offering various options ensures that all guests, including those with dietary restrictions, can enjoy the meal.

3. **Personalization:** Design signature cocktails that reflect your personalities or favorite drinks. You can even name them after significant places or events in your relationship.

4. **Guest Enjoyment:** Providing a unique cocktail experience can be a fun and memorable addition to your reception.

5. **Visual Appeal:** Pay attention to the presentation of the food. Beautifully plated dishes can elevate the dining experience and make it feel more special.

6. **Thematic Decor:** Use table settings and decor that complement your wedding theme, further enhancing the overall atmosphere.

These elements not only enhance the emotional significance of your wedding but also reflect your unique love story, ensuring a deeply personal and memorable celebration.

Cultural Fusions

Incorporating diverse cultural elements into your wedding celebration can create a truly unique and meaningful experience that honors your background and brings families together.

Bilingual Elements

Invitations

Create bilingual wedding invitations that honor both families' languages and cultures. Include translations for guests who may not be fluent in one language. Use cultural motifs and designs to enhance the aesthetic and meaning of the invitations.

Vows

Consider saying your vows in both languages during the ceremony. It's a beautiful way to express your love and commitment to each other while acknowledging your diverse backgrounds. This approach ensures that all guests, regardless of language, feel included in the ceremony.

Toasts

Encourage bilingual toasts during the reception. Family members and friends can share heartfelt messages in their native languages, creating a warm and inclusive atmosphere. This allows for the representation of different cultural expressions and sentiments.

Dual Ceremonies or Elements

If possible, have separate ceremonies representing each culture. For example, a Hindu ceremony followed by a Christian one. This allows you to celebrate both traditions fully. Each ceremony can include unique rituals and traditions, offering a rich experience for your guests.

Combine rituals from both cultures into one ceremony. For instance, incorporate elements like the unity candle lighting from Western weddings alongside a traditional tea ceremony from an Asian culture. Choose rituals that hold significant meaning in both cultures to create a harmonious blend.

Music and Dance

Include live music and dance performances from both cultures. Whether it's a traditional dance troupe or a fusion band, it adds vibrancy and excitement to the celebration. Live performances can highlight the event, providing entertainment and showcasing cultural heritage.

Encourage guests to join in cultural dances. Teach them simple steps during the reception, creating a joyful and interactive experience for everyone. This not only entertains guests but also engages them in the cultural aspects of the wedding.

Cultural Dress

Wear traditional attire from both cultures at different times during the wedding day. For example, you might wear a sari for the ceremony and a tuxedo or gown for the reception. This approach honors both cultural traditions and allows for a display of diverse heritage.

Culinary Delights

Create a menu that blends dishes from both cultures. Offer a variety of traditional foods that reflect your background, giving guests a taste of both worlds. Consider having food stations or a buffet that allows guests to explore and enjoy the diverse culinary offerings.

Rituals and Traditions

Incorporate various cultural rituals and traditions that are meaningful to you and your partner. This can include blessings, ceremonial dances, or symbolic acts that reflect your heritage. Explain these rituals in your program or through their officiant to help guests understand and appreciate their significance.

A multicultural wedding is an opportunity to celebrate diversity, honor your families' backgrounds, and create lasting memories for all. By thoughtfully blending elements from each culture, you can craft a wedding that is not only unique and personal but also a beautiful representation of your shared journey and the unity of your diverse backgrounds. Remember, the key is to balance and respect both cultures, creating an inclusive and memorable celebration for you and your guests.

Interactive Guest Activities

Infusing your wedding with interactive guest activities is an excellent way to add an extra layer of fun and engagement, ensuring that everyone has a memorable time celebrating your special day. Let's take a look at some creative ideas to entertain and delight your wedding guests (and yourself).

DIY Cocktail Bar

- **Mixology station:** Set up a DIY cocktail bar where guests can create their own signature drinks using a variety of spirits, mixers, and garnishes.

- **Recipe cards:** Provide recipe cards with suggested cocktail combinations or encourage guests to invent their own unique concoctions.

- **Bartender assistance:** Have a professional bartender or mixologist on hand to offer guidance and assistance, ensuring that even novice cocktail enthusiasts can craft delicious beverages.

Craft Corner

- **Creative crafts:** Create a craft corner stocked with supplies for guests to make personalized keepsakes, such as photo frames, mini scrapbooks, or custom coasters.

- **Instructional guides:** Offer simple craft tutorials or inspiration boards to spark creativity and help guests get started on their projects.

- **Collaborative art project:** Provide a communal canvas or large poster where guests can contribute their artistic talents, whether through thumbprints, handprints, or doodles, resulting in a unique piece of collaborative artwork.

Memory Lane

- **Photo booth:** Set up a photo booth with props and backdrops where guests can capture fun and memorable moments throughout the evening.

- **Memory lane display:** Create a "memory lane" display featuring photos and mementos from significant milestones in your relationship, inviting guests to reminisce and leave notes or well wishes.

- **Digital guestbook:** Offer a digital guestbook or interactive guestbook app where guests can leave virtual messages, photos, or videos that they can cherish long after the wedding day.

Interactive Games

- **Trivia challenges:** Host wedding-themed trivia games or quizzes during cocktail hour or dinner to entertain guests and test their knowledge of your relationship.

- **Giant lawn games:** Set up oversized lawn games like *Jenga*, *Cornhole*, or *Giant Connect Four* for guests to enjoy during outdoor receptions or cocktail hours.

- **Table games:** Place interactive table games or conversation starters at each table to encourage guests to mingle and interact throughout the evening.

Live Entertainment

- **Interactive performances:** Hire interactive entertainers such as magicians, caricature artists, or fortune tellers to engage guests and add a touch of whimsy to the festivities.

- **Live music requests:** Have a live band or DJ take song requests from guests, allowing them to personalize the music selection and keep the dance floor packed all night long.

These interactive elements will not only entertain your guests but also create lasting memories for you and your partner. By incorporating personalized and engaging activities, you can ensure that your wedding is a unique and unforgettable experience for everyone involved.

Chapter 5:

Staying Sane: Managing Stress and Enjoying the Journey

Wedding planning can often feel like a whirlwind of decisions, deadlines, and expectations, but fear not! You'll discover how to transform potential chaos into cherished moments.

Whether you're feeling overwhelmed by the endless to-do lists or seeking ways to stay centered amidst the flurry of activity, this chapter is your guide to finding balance, managing stress, and embracing the journey with a sense of calm and joy. Let's embark on this journey together and make your wedding planning experience as joyful as the day itself.

Stress Management Techniques

Wedding planning is undoubtedly a whirlwind of excitement, but it can also bring its fair share of stress. Make it a point to schedule regular downtime or "no wedding talk" days. Use this time to relax, indulge in hobbies, or spend quality time with loved ones, allowing yourself to recharge and find balance amidst the planning frenzy. Set boundaries by switching off wedding-related notifications during your designated downtime. This simple act can help you reclaim a sense of control and prevent wedding planning from taking over every aspect of your life.

Incorporate regular physical activity into your routine, whether it's yoga, jogging, or even just a leisurely stroll in nature. Exercise releases endorphins, the body's natural stress relievers, helping to alleviate tension and boost your overall mood.

Don't underestimate the power of a good night's sleep. Aim for consistent and sufficient sleep each night to recharge your body and mind, ensuring you're better equipped to handle the demands of wedding planning.

Integrate mindfulness exercises into your daily regimen to cultivate a sense of calm and clarity. Simple techniques like deep breathing exercises, meditation, or progressive muscle relaxation can help alleviate anxiety and promote relaxation.

Instead of getting caught up in future tasks or worrying about what's to come, focus on staying present in the moment. Mindfulness lets you center yourself and tackle challenges with a clear and composed mind.

Remember, prioritizing your mental and physical health throughout the wedding planning process is paramount. By incorporating these practical techniques into your routine, you can navigate the journey with greater ease, resilience, and enjoyment, ensuring that your wedding day remains a joyous and memorable occasion for all involved.

The Role of Support Systems

Involving friends and family in your wedding planning journey can infuse the process with a sense of togetherness and shared excitement. Here are some practical ways to enlist their help and make them an integral part of your special day.

Delegation Roles

Identify the unique strengths and interests of your friends and family members, then delegate tasks that align with their abilities and passions. Whether it's scouting for local transportation options, creating DIY decorations, or managing the guest list, involving loved ones in meaningful roles can make them feel valued and invested in your wedding day.

Communication Channels

Establish dedicated communication channels, such as group chats or regular meetings, to streamline wedding planning discussions and updates. These platforms facilitate collaboration, ensure everyone is on the same page, and minimize misunderstandings along the way.

Take advantage of wedding planning as an opportunity to bond with your parents and future in-laws. Treat yourselves to pampering activities like manicures, pedicures, or facials, creating cherished memories while simultaneously discussing wedding details in a relaxed and enjoyable setting.

Professional Help

While the support of family and friends is invaluable, there may be instances where professional guidance is necessary. Consider hiring a wedding planner or counselor to navigate any challenges or conflicts during the planning process. Their expertise and impartial perspective can help alleviate stress and ensure a smoother journey to your big day.

By striking a balance between involving loved ones in meaningful ways and seeking professional assistance when needed, you can harness the collective energy and enthusiasm of your support network while ensuring that your wedding planning experience remains both enjoyable and harmonious. Ultimately, the journey toward your special day becomes not just about the destination but also the shared moments and connections forged along the way.

Last-Minute Troubleshooting

You know it's not a complete wedding without some last-minute hiccups. Last-minute troubleshooting can be the saving grace for ensuring your wedding day runs smoothly.

Emergency Kit Preparation

Emergency kit preparation is a crucial aspect of wedding planning, ensuring you are equipped to handle any unexpected situations on your special day. Here are some common emergency kit checklists for your wedding day:

1. safety pins
2. double-sided fashion tape
3. sewing kit (needles, thread in various colors, scissors, buttons)
4. stain remover pen or wipes
5. backup makeup (lipstick, concealer, powder)
6. tissues
7. wet wipes
8. cash (small denominations)
9. band-Aids
10. pain reliever (such as ibuprofen or acetaminophen)
11. antacid tablets
12. breath mints or gum
13. snacks (granola bars, nuts, or dried fruit)
14. bottled water
15. small mirror
16. nail file
17. hair ties or bobby pins
18. deodorant wipes
19. hand sanitizer
20. portable phone charger
21. contact information for key vendors

22. list of important phone numbers (family, wedding party, venue, etc.)

23. copies of important documents (wedding timeline, contracts, etc.)

Remember to tailor this checklist to your specific needs and preferences, and consider any additional items that may be necessary based on your wedding venue, location, and activities planned for the day. Being prepared allows you to focus on enjoying the celebration without worrying about potential wardrobe malfunctions or other minor setbacks.

Vendor Backup Plans

Vendor backup plans involve collaborating with your vendors to establish contingency strategies in case of unforeseen circumstances. This proactive approach helps mitigate potential disruptions and ensures a smooth flow on your wedding day.

1. **Identify potential scenarios:** Sit down with your vendors and discuss potential scenarios that could arise, such as vendor cancellations due to illness or emergencies, transportation issues, equipment malfunctions, or weather-related challenges. By anticipating these possibilities, you can develop appropriate backup plans.

2. **Outline steps and responsibilities:** Once potential scenarios are identified, outline specific steps and responsibilities for both you and your vendors in addressing each situation. Clarify who will initiate the backup plan, what alternative arrangements will be made, and how communication will be managed.

3. **Secure backup contacts:** Obtain backup contact information for each vendor, including alternative phone numbers or email addresses. This ensures that you can reach them quickly in case of emergencies or last-minute changes.

4. **Confirm contingency measures:** Ensure that your vendors have contingency measures in place, such as access to backup equipment or personnel, alternative transportation options, or flexible scheduling arrangements. Verify that they are prepared to implement these measures if needed.

5. **Maintain open communication:** Regularly communicate with your vendors before the wedding day to keep them informed about any changes, updates, or concerns. Establish clear communication channels and encourage transparency to facilitate swift decision-making and problem-solving.

6. **Rehearse backup plans:** Consider conducting a rehearsal or walkthrough with your vendors to review the backup plans and ensure that everyone understands their roles and responsibilities. This rehearsal can help identify any potential gaps or issues that must be addressed before the wedding day.

By collaborating with your vendors to establish backup plans and maintaining open communication throughout the planning process, you can minimize the impact of unforeseen challenges and ensure a seamless and stress-free wedding day for you and your guests.

Mental Preparedness

Mental preparedness is essential for navigating the inevitable uncertainties of your wedding day with grace and resilience. Here's how to cultivate a mindset that allows you to embrace flexibility and maintain perspective:

1. **Embrace flexibility:** Recognize that despite meticulous planning, unforeseen events may occur. Prepare yourself mentally for the possibility that not everything will go exactly according to plan. Embracing flexibility allows you to adapt to changing circumstances with ease and poise.

2. **Focus on celebrating love and joy:** Keep the true essence of your wedding day at the forefront of your mind—celebrating your love and the joyous union with your partner. Amidst any challenges or hiccups, remind yourself of the significance of this momentous occasion, and let the love and happiness surrounding you guide your reactions.

3. **Maintain perspective:** When faced with minor setbacks or unexpected developments, maintain perspective by cherishing meaningful moments and embracing the presence of your loved ones. Remember that the essence of your wedding day lies in shared experiences, heartfelt connections, and joyous celebrations rather than in achieving perfection.

4. **Cultivate a positive mindset:** Adopt a positive mindset that empowers you to approach challenges with optimism and resilience. Trust in your ability to overcome obstacles and focus on finding solutions rather than dwelling on setbacks. By cultivating positivity, you can navigate any unexpected situation with confidence and grace.

5. **Implement preparedness measures:** Take proactive steps to prepare for potential challenges or emergencies, such as creating contingency plans and assembling emergency kits. Knowing that you have prepared for various scenarios can provide peace of mind and confidence in your ability to handle whatever comes your way.

With love, celebration, and resilience as your guiding principles, your wedding day will undoubtedly be beautiful, meaningful, and memorable, regardless of any challenges that may arise.

Reflecting and Celebrating

Wedding planning is a journey filled with excitement, but it can also be overwhelming at times. Reflecting and celebrating throughout your wedding planning journey is essential for maintaining joy and connection amidst the whirlwind of tasks and decisions.

Journaling the Journey

Keeping a dedicated wedding journal allows you to capture the emotions, milestones, and reflections that accompany the planning process. Take time to write about your experiences, challenges, and moments of joy. Not only does journaling serve as a therapeutic outlet for stress, but it also creates a tangible record of your journey to cherish in the years to come.

Celebratory Rituals

Celebrate each milestone and achievement in your wedding planning journey with special rituals or treats. Whether it's securing a venue, finalizing the guest list, or completing DIY projects, mark these occasions with moments of celebration and gratitude. Treat yourselves to a romantic dinner, indulge in a spa day, or simply enjoy a quiet evening together. These rituals acknowledge your progress and strengthen your bond as a couple.

Staying Connected With Your Partner

Amidst the hustle and bustle of wedding preparations, prioritize quality time with your partner. Set aside regular check-ins where you can focus on each other, away from wedding-related stressors. Share your hopes, dreams, and fears, laugh together, and reaffirm your commitment to one another. Remember that your relationship is the foundation of your wedding journey, so nurturing it along the way is crucial for a joyful and meaningful experience.

Embracing the Journey

Embrace the entire wedding planning process as a journey of love, growth, and shared dreams. Treasure each step along the way, from the excitement of engagement to the joy of exchanging vows. Embrace both the challenges and the triumphs, knowing that each moment contributes to the beautiful tapestry of your love story. By savoring the journey together with your partner, you can create lasting memories and deepen your connection as you prepare for your special day.

Incorporating these practices into your wedding planning journey allows you to navigate the process with joy, connection, and appreciation for the love that brings you together. Embrace the experience, celebrate the milestones, and cherish every moment as you prepare to embark on this new chapter of your lives together.

Conclusion

As you stand on the threshold of your wedding day, take a moment to reflect on the incredible journey you've undertaken. Every decision made, every laugh shared, and every dream realized have been woven together to create the intricate tapestry of your unique love story.

Amidst the whirlwind of excitement and anticipation surrounding your wedding day, it's crucial to acknowledge that the journey leading up to it may not unfold exactly as planned. Like any adventure worth embarking upon, the path to your wedding day may be dotted with unexpected twists and turns. However, rather than viewing these challenges as stumbling blocks, consider them as opportunities for growth and transformation.

Embracing the unexpected with grace allows you to infuse your love story with depth and richness. Just as a tapestry gains texture and beauty from its intricate patterns, so too does your relationship flourish when tested by the unforeseen. Each obstacle navigated and hurdle overcome becomes a chapter in your love story, illustrating the strength of your bond and your ability to overcome adversity together.

Resilience becomes your greatest ally as you encounter bumps along the road. It empowers you to weather storms with unwavering determination and to emerge stronger on the other side. Rather than allowing setbacks to derail your plans, resilience encourages you to adapt, improvise, and find creative solutions to any challenges that arise.

Creativity also plays an important role in transforming obstacles into opportunities. It prompts you to think outside the box, explore unconventional solutions, and infuse your wedding journey with your unique flair and personality. From improvising alternative arrangements to incorporating unexpected elements into your celebration, creativity allows you to turn setbacks into memorable moments that add depth and character to your love story.

And amidst it all, a touch of magic weaves its way through the fabric of your wedding journey. It's the intangible spark that ignites when you face challenges with optimism, find joy in the little moments, and trust in the power of love to guide you through even the darkest of times. This magic infuses your relationship with hope, resilience, and an unwavering belief in the beauty of your shared journey.

So, as you navigate the twists and turns on the path to your wedding day, remember that it's not the smoothness of the road that defines your love story but rather the grace, resilience, creativity, and touch of magic with which you navigate it. With these qualities as your compass, you'll not only overcome any challenges that come your way but also emerge stronger, more united, and ready to embark on the next chapter of your journey together.

As you embark on this journey, surrounded by the love and support of your family and friends, know that you are never alone. Their joy, tears, and unwavering presence form a beautiful tapestry of love that will envelop you on your special day.

If this guide has been helpful in your wedding planning journey, I would be deeply grateful if you shared your thoughts and experiences through a review. Your feedback fuels my passion and helps future couples find their way to their own happily ever afters.

And now, as you prepare to step into forever with your beloved, may your wedding day be a radiant celebration of love, laughter, and the beautiful imperfections that make your story uniquely yours. Here's to your happily ever after!

References

Bradley, K. (2022). *Five easy tips to remember when planning a wedding menu.* 7 Centerpieces. https://www.7centerpieces.com/planning/five-easy-tips-to-remember-when-planning-a-wedding-menu/

Brides Editors. (2022, November 28). *Wedding cost checklist: here's how to allocate your entire wedding budget.* Brides. https://www.brides.com/story/wedding-budget-guide-allocating-funds-staying-on-track

Bronstein, P. (2022, July 29). *Tips on how to enjoy the wedding planning process.* Thewed. https://thewed.com/magazine/tips-on-how-to-enjoy-the-wedding-planning-process

Charlotte. (2022, October 26). *DIY vs all inclusive weddings - what's best for you?* Wedinspire. https://www.wedinspire.com/articles/guide/diy-vs-all-inclusive-weddings-whats-best-for-you/

Chertoff, A. (2017, July 20). *11 tips to help you plan a multicultural wedding.* Wedding Wire. https://www.weddingwire.com/wedding-ideas/plan-a-multicultural-wedding

Chertoff, J., & Darling, G. (2023). *75 wedding themes to inspire every type of couple.* Zola. https://www.zola.com/expert-advice/wedding-themes

Choosing your wedding colours according to their meaning. (2014, November 5). Bride Online. https://brideonline.com.au/wedding-decorations-and-hire/choosing-your-wedding-colours-according-to-their-meaning/

Claire. (2019, November 11). *Tips & tools: How to deal with wedding anxiety and planning stress.* One Fab Day. https://onefabday.com/wedding-anxiety-stress/

Cockett, S. (2019, March 7). *The ultimate guide to wedding themes: inspirational planning ideas.* Hitched. https://www.hitched.co.uk/wedding-planning/organising-and-planning/a-guide-to-wedding-themes/

D, T. (2022, April 19). *45 fun wedding reception activities & wedding games.* Zazzle Ideas. https://www.zazzle.com/ideas/wedding/wedding-reception-activities-wedding-games

deBara, D. (2022, January 10). *42 unique wedding traditions around the world.* Zola. https://www.zola.com/expert-advice/how-couples-are-integrating-culture-into-their-weddings-in-2022

DiBlasi, C. E. (2021, February 26). *14 cultural wedding traditions you might not have seen before.* Bridal Musings. https://bridalmusings.com/171746/cultural-wedding-traditions-you-might-not-have-seen-before/

Donovan, B. (2023, August 21). *23 wedding theme ideas for any style.* Brides. https://www.brides.com/story/wedding-themes-for-every-bridal-style

Elizabeth, C. (2019, November 12). *4 tips for finding destination wedding vendors.* Cavin Elizabeth Photography. https://www.cavinelizabeth.com/wedding-planning-tips/4-tips-finding-destination-wedding-vendors/

15 critical tips for managing your wedding guest list. (2018). Wedding Spot Blog. https://www.weddingspot.com/blog/tips-managing-wedding-guest-list

Forrest, K. (2015, April 27). *How much does the average wedding cost, according to data?* The Knot. https://www.theknot.com/content/average-wedding-cost

Forrest, K. (2021, February 25). *7 ways to reduce wedding-planning stress, from a meditation expert*. Wedding Wire. https://www.weddingwire.com/wedding-ideas/10-ways-to-reduce-stress-during-wedding-planning

Forrest, K. (2022, January 18). *Everything you need to know about your wedding party and their responsibilities*. The Knot. https://www.theknot.com/content/wedding-party-glossary

How to choose a wedding theme that fits your personality. (2024). Transaction Transportation. https://www.transactiontransportation.com/how-to-choose-a-wedding-theme-that-fits-your-personality

How to find your wedding style. (2024). Here Comes the Guide. https://www.herecomestheguide.com/wedding-ideas/how-to-find-your-wedding-style

How your friends play an important role in your wedding. (2022, January 20). Portfolio Studio. https://www.portfoliostudio.in/how-your-friends-play-an-important-role-in-your-wedding/

Hurst, A. (2024, March 21). *Average cost of a wedding: by state and feature*. Value Penguin. https://www.valuepenguin.com/average-cost-of-wedding

Johnson, C. (2016, August 4). *Multicultural wedding planning advice from 17 real newlyweds*. The Knot. https://www.theknot.com/content/multicultural-wedding-tips

Kaitlyn. (2019, May 17). *Honoring culture & heritage in your wedding: tips from Chancey Charm*. Brides of Houston. https://houston.wedsociety.com/article/honoring-culture-heritage-wedding/

Keegan, S. (2021a, July 27). *How to incorporate your culture in your wedding*. https://stephaniekeegan.com/how-to-incorporate-your-culture-in-your-wedding/

Keegan, S. (2021b, July 27). *How to incorporate your culture in your wedding*. https://stephaniekeegan.com/how-to-incorporate-your-culture-in-your-wedding/

Kellogg, K., Taylor, E., Boutayna Chokrane, & Van Zanten, V. (2023, November 2). *Wedding budget breakdown: How to calculate and budget wedding costs*. Vogue. https://www.vogue.com/article/wedding-budget-planning-calculator-guide

Lake, R. (2022, April 12). *How to save and plan for a wedding*. Investopedia. https://www.investopedia.com/financial-edge/0212/how-to-save-for-a-wedding.aspx

Levine, N. G. (2024, February 16). *40 signature drink ideas for your wedding*. Wezoree. https://wezoree.com/inspiration/40-signature-drink-ideas-your-wedding/

List of wedding roles: know the different roles in a wedding. (2021). Villalaestancia. https://rivieranayarit.villalaestancia.com/blog/weddings/list-of-wedding-roles

Lord, M. (2016, October 27). *What to DIY at a wedding and what not to.* Rustic Wedding Chic. https://rusticweddingchic.com/what-to-diy-at-a-wedding-and-what-not-to-do-yourself

Lord, M. (2023, November 11). *88 best wedding themes for 2024 for any taste and style.* Wedding Forward. https://www.weddingforward.com/wedding-themes/

Macleod, M. (2022, November 2). *Wedding planning stress: 13 ways to look after yourself & reduce stress.* Hitched. https://www.hitched.co.uk/wedding-planning/organising-and-planning/wedding-stress-management/

Mitchell, E. (2022, October 30). *Avoid these 10 mistakes when choosing your wedding color palette.* Brides. https://www.brides.com/story/wedding-color-palette-mistakes

Monique, J. (2019, November 4). *A guide on how to choose a wedding theme.* The Brillianteers. https://www.brillianteers.com/blog/a-guide-to-choosing-a-wedding-theme

Montemayor, C. (2020). *8 sample wedding ceremony scripts to guide your own celebration.* Brides. https://www.brides.com/wedding-ceremony-script-5074157

Mulvey, K. (2023, February 2). *How to set boundaries with your family while wedding planning.* Brides. https://www.brides.com/boundaries-family-wedding-planning-6502440

Murtaugh, T. (2015). *27 ideas for including your wedding guests in the party of a lifetime.* Martha Stewart. https://www.marthastewart.com/7865359/ideas-including-wedding-guests-party-lifetime

Nowack, H. (2008a, May 15). *The ultimate guide to incorporating multiple cultures into your wedding.* The Knot. https://www.theknot.com/content/incorporating-multiple-cultures-into-your-wedding

Nowack, H. (2008b, May 16). *What your wedding budget should look like, according to data.* The Knot. https://www.theknot.com/content/wedding-budget-ways-to-save-money

Nowack, H. (2016a, May 10). *How to plan an affordable wedding, according to experts.* The Knot. https://www.theknot.com/content/wedding-budget-tips

Nowack, H. (2016b, October 21). *25 amazing wedding themes that stand the test of time.* The Knot. https://www.theknot.com/content/wedding-theme-ideas

O'Connell, B. (2018, August 28). *How much does a wedding cost on average (with breakdown)?* The Street. https://www.thestreet.com/personal-finance/how-much-does-wedding-cost-14693474

Riley. (2021, January 22). *10 tips to beat wedding planning stress.* Junebug Weddings. https://junebugweddings.com/wedding-blog/beat-wedding-planning-stress-with-these-10-cool-tips/

Ryan, L. (2022, July 29). *Wedding planning stress? Here's how to enjoy the experience.* Brides. https://www.brides.com/wedding-planning-stress-experts-enjoying-the-experience-5204954

Sarah. (2019, July 10). *Seven colors with hidden meanings to include in your wedding color scheme.* Bridesmaid. https://www.bridesmaid.com/blog/post/2019/07/10/seven-colors-with-hidden-meanings-to-include-in-your-wedding-color-scheme

Schreiber, S. (2024, February 14). *50 tried-and-true wedding color schemes to inspire your own*. Martha Stewart. https://www.marthastewart.com/7933433/choosing-wedding-color-palette

Schwahn, L. (2024, May 6). *How much does the average wedding cost?* NerdWallet. https://www.nerdwallet.com/article/finance/how-much-does-average-wedding-cost

Seona. (2016, December 7). *DIY wedding playlist or hire a professional wedding DJ*. Rob Alberti Event Services. https://robalberti.com/diy-wedding-playlist-hire-professional-wedding-dj/

7 colours with secret meanings for your wedding colour scheme. (2023, January 7). Nabbd. https://nabbd.co.uk/seven-colours-secret-meanings-wedding-colour-scheme/

Skorobohatykh, O. (2023, March 27). *How to choose wedding colors: Secret tips and tricks*. Wedding Forward. https://www.weddingforward.com/how-to-choose-wedding-colors/

Strasberg Roysso, K. (2024, April 30). *95 wedding vow examples that will melt your heart*. Southern Living. https://www.southernliving.com/weddings/wedding-vow-examples

10 tips for vetting your wedding vendors so there are no regrets – the ring boxes. (2024). The Ring Boxes. https://www.theringboxes.com/blogs/wedding-planning/vetting-vendors

37 ways to save money on your wedding | cheap wedding ideas. (2024). Here Comes the Guide. https://www.herecomestheguide.com/wedding-ideas/how-to-save-money-on-wedding

Thompson, Z. (2019, July 14). *How to have a multicultural wedding*. TLC. https://www.tlc.com/weddings/ways-to-make-your-multicultural-wedding-memorable

Tigar, L. (2021, June 23). *How to give up control during wedding planning and just enjoy the process*. Wedding Wire. https://www.weddingwire.com/wedding-ideas/type-a-wedding-planning

Title, S. (2017, February 16). *7 things that are fun about wedding planning*. Wedding Wire. https://www.weddingwire.com/wedding-ideas/7-things-that-are-fun-about-wedding-planning

Traditional wedding ceremony and wedding vows. (2017). Lake Tahoe Weddings. https://www.laketahoeweddings.net/wedding-vows/traditional-wedding-ceremony-and-vows/

12 things a smart bride should and should never DIY. (2017, January 20). WedSites. https://blog.wedsites.com/12-things-smart-bride-never-diy/

Wedding day hacks: 5 common problems and how to prevent them. (2023, June 24). Rocket Lawyer. https://www.rocketlawyer.com/family-and-personal/family-matters/marriage/legal-guide/how-to-prevent-common-wedding-day-problems

Wedding guest list management. (2024). WedSites. https://wedsites.com/guest-list-management

What is a DIY wedding? And should I have one? (2020, January 21). Hargate Hall. https://www.hargate-hall.co.uk/what-is-a-diy-wedding-and-should-i-have-one/

Made in the USA
Las Vegas, NV
18 April 2025